The Promise

&

The Process

How to hang on to hope and grow through the journey

Tyler Sollie

The Promise and The Process

How to hang on to hope as you grow through the journey

Copyright © 2019 Tyler Sollie

ISBN: 9781706813200

DEDICATION

To Judah, Justus and Faith:

You are the greatest blessings your Mom and I have ever experienced outside of the grace of Jesus.

Remember this: God's promise for you is BIG. God's promise for you is REAL. Seeing those promises come to pass in your life will more often than not include a process. The process might be different than what you expected. But be sure of this, it is worth it. And never lose sight of the fact that Jesus will be with you every step of the way.

What you will grow to find over time is that His promises are not just about us and for us as individuals, but He wants to allow our journey to bring hope, life and transformation to many people around us. In other words, He allows us to be a part of His great mission.

Never let go of His promise. Never back away from the process.

Never give up.

I love you.

Dad

Tyler Sollie

CONTENTS

ACKNOWLEDGMENTS

There have been many people who have served as encouraging voices throughout the journey of putting this idea to paper. Thank you to David Hertweck and many other friends who took time to read, give feedback, help edit, critique and ultimately make a better book than I could have made by myself. There is strength in numbers, and you have been a source of strength to me!

Thank you to the pastors and team at Life Center. You have brought so much encouragement and inspiration throughout the journey. This book sat unfinished through a season of challenge. I am so thankful for those who encouraged me to pick it up and continue to write, even as we navigated our own "process of growth" at Life Center. I am thankful for you and love that we get to do this *together*.

Thank you to my parents, Tim and Marcia Sollie, for always supporting me, believing in me and most importantly, praying for me. I love you.

A special thank you to my wife Amber. Your partnership means more than you know. Thank you for listening to my ideas, thoughts and all of my "thinking out loud" moments. Your patience, encouragement and support mean more than you will ever know.

DON'T AVOID THE PROCESS

INTRODUCTION

Don't Avoid the Process

I like to avoid pain. Like, at all costs. Who doesn't? In fact, there have been times in my life that I have been accused of being an "over reactor". Can you believe that? Me? An *over reactor?* The crazy thing is I wouldn't have believed it if I hadn't had kids of my own. As they have grown, I can see little parts of myself in them. I can see reactions that they do, and I know where they got them from: their MOTHER! Ok. Ok. – they absolutely got those reactions from me. But here is the point: none of us enjoy pain. We look to minimize it if at all possible. Most of us don't sign up for doing things that lead us to a place of discomfort. That is, unless we see the value of enduring the challenge.

A number of years ago, a friend got me into cycling. To be honest, I never thought I would ever be "one of those guys" who puts on the spandex and rides a bicycle around for *fun*. But in the words of the great poet Justin Bieber: "Never say Never". So there I was, a road bike, a pair of padded spandex shorts and miles and miles of road in the Pacific Northwest. It started small: a 10 mile ride and then a 15 mile ride. After a few months I worked myself up to doing my first 40 mile ride from our home at the time on the eastside of Seattle to Century Link Field and back (Go Seahawks!).

I thought I was going to die.

That was the hardest thing I had ever done physically in my life up to that point. But then something crazy happened: I recovered. And I was ready to push myself even farther.

A few summers ago, three friends and I did the Seattle to Portland ride. This is an annual ride where around 10,000 cyclists from around the world make the journey south, leaving the University of Washington in Seattle, and ending in downtown Portland. We trained for months. Rain or shine (obviously more rain than sun here in the Northwest) we had to put in miles on our bikes. Why did we do it? Why go through all that pain and discomfort? It wasn't because we had a hunger to be miserable. No, it was because of the goal. That summer the four of us were going to do the Seattle to Portland, all 205 miles of it, *in one day.*

Crazy?

Absolutely.

Worth it?

Without a doubt.

If we were asked to make a decision between effort and ease, most of us would instantly opt for ease. It is in our nature. It makes sense, doesn't it? The world around us often yells that comfort is king. Work for the weekend. Press hard through the monotony of life so that you can *finally* arrive at retirement. Then you get to live the real life you have always wanted. The desire for comfort isn't wrong in and of itself, until it gets in the way of something more important in our lives. The danger, however, is when our appetite for comfort kills our willingness to endure the process. As I approach my 40's (yes, I just winced a little when I typed that out), I am learning that more often than not, God has used the journey of a *process* in my life. My guess is that if you took a closer look at your life, you would see His hand in the midst of your journey as well.

> # THE DANGER IS WHEN OUR APPETITE FOR COMFORT KILLS OUR WILLINGNESS TO ENDURE THE PROCESS.

We can all remember times in our lives when we had a grand dream about what the future would hold. Nothing could hold us back or stop us from what we *knew* was going to be our destiny. But most of us have experienced the slap of life. We encounter a reality check that we weren't looking for and we definitely didn't sign up for. All of the sudden, the dream that seemed so close, so real and so beautiful, feels like a 500 mile walk away. Can you relate? If so, this book is for you.

In the pages ahead, we are going to read about a young man named Joseph. He had a big dream, what I would call a Promise. The Promise included this place called a Palace. Here was the tension though: between the Promise and the Palace, there was a Process. The process that Joseph faced can be read in the bible in Genesis 37-47. As we will discover, my guess is that there were times when he asked himself, "Where is God in all of *this*?"

WHERE IS GOD IN ALL OF THIS?

Like Joseph, we have all faced or will face stuff that we didn't sign up for. A disappointing diagnosis. An unexpected detour. Some unrequested discouragement and misunderstandings. A dead end that we didn't see on the map we were following. If we are not careful, these pieces of the process can be seen as God losing sight of us, or worse, that God has somehow abandoned us or broken His promise to us.

We will soon discover that delay doesn't necessarily mean denial. Just because it didn't happen or isn't happening like you planned or thought it would go, that doesn't mean that it isn't going to happen. Here is some good news for all of us: Jesus is always faithful, even when we are unable to see past the current circumstance that we find ourselves in right now. What we might feel is our defining moment, God may simply see as a small step in the process that He is right alongside of us in. For Joseph, between the Promise and the Palace included many steps along the way: the Pit, the Pressure, the

Prison…it was all a part of the process, preparing and cultivating Joseph so that he would be ready for the Palace.

Lean into the process. Few people rarely jump from the promise right to the palace. As we journey together though the following chapters I want to encourage you to consider the places you have been along the journey.

Where have you wanted to toss in the towel and give up?

Where were the detours that you were certain that they were not supposed to be there?

What are you facing right now that is screaming at you that you can't make it or that God has forgotten about you?

If you are there, or have been there, you are in good company. Our friend Joseph has experienced some of those same realities. Let's take a moment to get a little more acquainted with him…

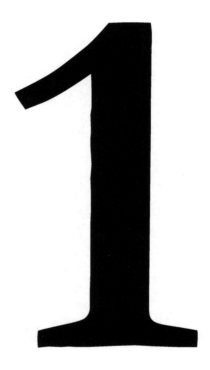

Chapter 1: **WHO IS JOSEPH?**

Technicolor challenges

I remember in elementary school the divisions of people within any given class room. From the first day of school in early September, while the sun was still warm in western Washington, kids would begin to take account of who was around them and how they fit into the social structure. There were the funny kids. They had the attention of the whole class. They seemed to know the key ingredient of humor, like it was embedded into their DNA as a gift from God himself. There were the athletic kids. These guys and girls were always the captains of whatever you were doing at recess. They would line all the other kids up as they stood there, hoping and praying that they would not be the last ones picked yet once again. Please, don't ask me how I know this detail. There were also the cool kids or the influencers. These kids were the trend setters. Though they might have not been physically big, when they walked into the cafeteria or down the breezeway toward the school bus pick up, people took notice.

There was another specific type of kid that I remember from my elementary school years. Every class seemed to have one. They brought a certain level of distain and angst with them, not just because what they did, but often because of *how* they did it. That's right. I'm talking about the teacher's pet.

These kids seemed like they could do no wrong. They got all the special treatment. Guess who the line leader was? Them. Guess who got called on to run a message to the office? Them. Guess who was *always* picked first to play 'Heads Up 7 Up' during rainy day recess? You got it, the teacher's pet. No one wanted to be them, but everyone wanted to have the treatment that they received. Why? Because they were treated special. They seemed to have some unspoken favor from the person with all of the power, the teacher. And it is this very frustration and tension that we see about Joseph when he arrives on the scene.

AN IMPERFECT, IMPORTANT FAMILY STORY

So who exactly is this guy named Joseph? In Genesis 37 we see him enter the storyline of scripture:

> "*So Jacob settled again in the land of Canaan, where his father had lived as a foreigner. This is the account of Jacob and his family. When Joseph was seventeen years old, he often tended his father's flocks. He worked for his half brothers, the sons of his father's wives Bilhah and Zilpah. But Joseph reported to his father some of the bad things his brothers were doing.* **Jacob loved Joseph more than any of his other children because Joseph had been born to him in his old age.** *So one day Jacob had a special gift made for Joseph—a beautiful robe. But his brothers hated Joseph because their father loved him more than the rest of them. They couldn't say a kind word to him.*" (Genesis 37:1–4, NLT – emphasis added)

This family, with all of its dysfunction (more on that in a bit), was central to God's great rescue plan to bring salvation to the world. Earlier in Genesis God revealed himself to a man named Abram who would later have his name changed to Abraham. If you grew

19

up in church, you most likely sang a song about him being your father – which if you are like me caused me great confusion because my father's name is Tim. But back to the story: God tells Abraham that he has been chosen and that God is going to make a covenant with him and his family *to be a blessing*.

> *"The* LORD *had said to Abram, "Leave your native country, your relatives, and your father's family, and go to the land that I will show you. I will make you into a great nation. I will bless you and make you famous, and you will be a blessing to others. I will bless those who bless you and curse those who treat you with contempt.* **All the families on earth will be blessed through you.***"''* (Genesis 12:1–3, NLT)

How cool is that? God chose Abraham and his family to be a blessing to *all* the families of the earth! Cue the celebration music and the confetti. There was only one problem: Abraham and his wife Sarah didn't have any kids. To make matters even more bleak, they were old – *very* old. But from the truth of this story were learn something extremely important about the character and nature of God: His is always faithful to fulfill *His* promises. It just doesn't always happen in the way we think it will or should happen.

As the story continues, Abraham and his wife have a son through God's provision (they tried to make it happen through their own effort and ideas, which led to a lot of pain and heartache – which usually happens when we try and take matters into our own hands). This son was named Isaac. As Isaac grows, he gets married and he and his wife have twin sons: Esau and Jacob. As we read this story we keep waiting to see how God is going to fulfill this great promise of blessing through the family, but there is more dysfunction.

Jacob deceives his dad and steals Esau's blessing, which was rightfully his as the firstborn son. It's a crazy story! He uses animal hair to disguise who he really is since Esau was hairy and he wasn't. This is totally where reality TV could have had its start! Jacob runs for his life, ends up working for years to receive his wife, only to be deceived himself. Eventually, after years have passed, Jacob again meets his brother and you are expecting the ultimate cage match, but instead Esau is gracious to Jacob who shortly after has his name changed by God to Israel. Jacob (who is now known as Israel) had a lot of children, one of whom was born to him in his old age. You guessed it! Joseph.

It is vital to start with the perspective of the family and the Promise that God made in order to understand the significance of Joseph's journey. He has a key role to play in the world coming to experience this great blessing that God talked to Abraham about, a blessing that is ultimately fulfilled through the life, death and resurrection of Jesus. But things go sideways thanks to that technicolor coat and the special treatment that he got from his dad. Things for Joseph are about to take an unexpected turn.

When I was younger I had always wished that I had an older brother. Don't get me wrong, I LOVE my sister Tasha and I am thankful for her every single day. But I remember as a child thinking how cool it would be to have a tough older brother. Someone who would stick up for me, help me build my biceps and even let me ride with him in his car. It never happened. It wasn't until I read this story in Genesis a little later in life that I was thankful that God didn't give me an older brother, let alone *eleven* of them. It is one thing to be picked on by an older brother but imagine taking on an entire football team by yourself. This is what Joseph is living with.

As Joseph's story opens, we see a 17-year-old teenager who feels like he is ready to take on the world in front of him. He was young, spoiled by his father and, as we are about to see, was going to have to experience a lot of life in order to get him ready for the role that he was going to play in this great rescue plan that God had in place for the world. For Joseph, the process that would prepare him for the role he would play all started with a dream.

A *big* dream.

Chapter 2: **The PROMISE**

God has a big vision and a big dream, for ME... kind of

As a dad of 3 children, I always love it when they share some of their big dreams that they have for their future. One of my most prized possessions is a piece of artwork drawn and colored by my son Justus. This treasure hangs on the wall of my home office and every time that I look at it I smile and think to myself, I never want to stop dreaming and creating like a child. When Justus was in the 2nd grade I asked him to take a blank piece of paper and color something for me. I told him it could be *anything* he wanted. He took some crayons and that piece of paper and disappeared for a while. Eventually he came into my office and revealed the treasure that he had been working on. As he began to explain his masterpiece to me, I sat in awe at the creativity and clarity that he had put to paper. Where did all this creativity come from? How did he come up with this so quickly? And why can't I color as good as my 2nd grade son?

The picture was a rocket ship with three windows, each window having a person looking out the window with excitement and joy with what they were about to experience. The rocket ship was taking off from some distant grey planet, with countless stars in the distance and a universe of possibilities awaiting it. When I asked him who the three individuals were in the windows he replied, "This one is my best friend...the one in the middle window is me, and that other guy... that is you Daddy." I quickly looked for a box of tissues, explaining to him that my allergies must be kicking up again. There are so many reasons that I love and treasure that picture. But one of the biggest reasons is that of all the things he could have drawn – of all the possibilities and potentials there could have been, he saw a big dream and included *me* in it! At times I find myself looking at the picture and praying a simple prayer: "Jesus, help me to never lose my creativity, and childlike ability to dream."

WHAT IS YOUR ROCKET SHIP?

Somewhere along the line, many of us tend to lose our ability to dream big. We allow reality to slap us in the face enough times to "know better". We look at our crayon colored dreams of our childhood and say to ourselves there is no way that can ever happen. Maybe when you were younger you had a grand vision of what your life would look like. You saw a never-ending series of adventure and excitement. But now, maybe a few decades into life, you realize that things didn't pan out the way you thought they would. You keep hoping that someday you will wake up and find yourself in the adventure that you had always hoped for, but ultimately you know better than that now. You have convinced yourself there is no point to keep that dream alive.

Some of us had a dream to impact our world. To shape culture, art, music, technology or medicine. We had a dream to use our days not just trying to survive, but using them to do something great, and maybe even *be* someone great. The rocket ship was real, and we were going to build it and bring others along with us. But then something happened. We were told it would never happen. We experienced a dead end or a setback. Our priorities were adjusted for us with unforeseen circumstances that we were not planning on and we didn't sign up for. Maybe we convinced ourselves that *eventually* we will get to it, just not right now. Maybe the rocket ship *was* real and *is* real. Maybe we just lost sight of it. Or maybe it had a different purpose than we realized.

JOSEPH'S BIG DREAM

So, let's get back to our friend named Joseph. In Genesis 37 Joseph is around 17 years old and we read about the day that he had a dream. This dream is so incredible, and he is so excited about it that he decides to share it with his family, because that is what you do with awesome dreams...you share them with other people, right? What is the point of having an amazing dream if you can't tell everyone about it? By the way, don't we all do this? I still tell my friends and family about cool, scary or funny dreams that I have.

What is interesting about Joseph is that he thought he understood his dream and what his dream meant. He was so confident about it. Listen to the language used about *his* dream and what *he assumed* his dream was all about:

*"**One night Joseph had a dream**, and when he told his brothers about it, they hated him more than ever. "Listen to this dream," he said. "We were out in the field, tying up bundles of grain. Suddenly my bundle stood up, and your bundles all gathered around and bowed low before mine!" His brothers responded, "So you think you will be our king, do you? Do you actually think you will reign over us?" And they hated him all the more because of his dreams and the way he talked about them. **Soon Joseph had another dream**, and again he told his brothers about it. "Listen, I have had another dream," he said. "The sun, moon, and eleven stars bowed low before me!" This time he told the dream to his father as well as to his brothers, but his father scolded him. "What kind of dream is that?" he asked. "Will your mother and I and your brothers actually come and bow to the ground before you?" But while his brothers were jealous of Joseph, his father wondered what the dreams meant."* (Genesis 37:5–11, NLT)

There are a few things we can learn about this dream. First, it seems that Joseph didn't just see this as one of those "I had too much pizza" type of dreams. To him, this dream seemed like it had a *promise* attached to it. In other words, Joseph believed that this was more than just something that randomly happened one night in his sleep. He saw this as a part of his destiny. Somehow, some way, someday this thing was going to happen. We learn later on that this in fact was a promise given by God for his future. We will see in the chapters ahead just how accurate this dream was and how every part of this dream would come to pass.

Second, we learn that not everyone will love and value the dream. In this story we see Joseph share his dream with his brothers who were already uptight about this spoiled and favored younger brother of theirs. Things don't get better when he shares this dream. Just the opposite happens. His brothers end up "hating him more than ever." Have you ever had someone get upset at you *because* of a dream?

Not too long ago I woke up one morning completely mad and frustrated at Amber. I couldn't believe what she had said to me *in my dream* the night before. I actually expected an apology from her the next morning. The crazy thing is, I didn't get one! Can you believe that? As crazy as that sounds, it is true. It wasn't her fault that I had dreamt that she said what she said. She wasn't responsible for an apology. She didn't cause the dream…the pizza did!

Not everyone will believe your dream.

Not everyone will appreciate your dream.

Not everyone will encourage your dream.

You have to be okay with that. Here is why: if it is a God-given dream and promise, it *will* come to pass. It probably will not happen tomorrow, or the day after. As we will soon come to find, seeing God's dream for our lives take place usually happens through a *process*. Joseph will soon find out that holding on to the truth of this dream will be important as he navigates the challenges that are waiting for him in the seasons ahead.

The third truth we learn from this dream is how we communicate things matters. There was something in the way that Joseph communicated this dream that enraged his brothers. He soon has another dream, and that one ticked his parents off too. Remember that old saying, "It's not just *what* you say, but *how* you say it?" That could have potentially saved Joseph some pain if he would have seen that bumper sticker on the back of a camel. Here is the challenge for young Joseph: He really did dream this. But how he communicated this dream revealed that he didn't yet fully understand how God was going to use him to see this dream come to pass.

THE DREAM IS ABOUT ME, RIGHT?

The summer between 7th and 8th grade I had a
chance to go to summer camp with my church. I
remember being so excited to be away from home for
a week, hanging out with friends, swimming, eating
candy all day every day and of course, spending time
getting closer to God…(I knew the right things to
say, even back then). It was a life changing week! In
the midst of all the fun, all the games and all the
memories that I was making, God showed up and
revealed Himself to me in a way that I had never
experienced in my life up to that point. Right there,
in that chapel at Cedar Springs Camp in western
Washington, I actually felt like God spoke to *me*.
Who was I that I would have God's attention to the
point that He would want to speak to me?

That night at camp, as I was preparing to go into
the 7th grade, I felt Jesus tell me that someday I was
going to be a youth pastor! I was beyond excited. I
didn't really know all that it meant – but I knew
where I was headed. I felt like God had given me a
dream. I had received a *promise* over my life. Little
did I know all that would be required of me to see
that promise come to fulfillment. I remember
spending the last few days at camp walking around
with my head a little higher, my chest out in front of
me thinking "God spoke to *me*. He called *me*. I *must be*

important!" Even though my words might not have been expressing these thoughts, my mind and heart were screaming this!

Here was the problem: I thought it was about *me*. Yes, I believe that Jesus really did speak to me. He opened the doors for me, provided mentors who helped to shape and prepare me, He led me through jr. high, high school and college helping to keep that call and dream in front of me. I remember the day that I started as a youth pastor at Eastridge Church in Issaquah, Washington, thinking to myself, "It really happened!" But the journey from the dream at camp to my first day as a youth pastor included a process of preparation that I didn't know would be included.

A number of years ago, I was asked to speak to a local church school of ministry. I remember praying about what I should share with this group of excited and eager young leaders. Many of these young adults felt a God-given dream in their lives to serve others through local church ministry. One area that I knew many young leaders wrestled with was navigating the season between "feeling called" and seeing the fulfillment. In other words, they were navigating the same tension that Joseph experienced. The *promise* was real. But it didn't happen the next day.

I remember sharing with that group of young leaders that there was something significant that God was doing in the life of Joseph. Just as they had a dream in their heart from God, so did Joseph. But God was going to grow and prepare Joseph through the process. Just because He had received the promise, didn't mean that he was quite ready to walk in it. He needed to grow through the process that God was going to allow him to experience. I reminded these students, just like I want to remind you, that God is preparing each of us. God allowed the process, not only to prepare Joseph, but to help him understand that the *promise* wasn't really about *him*.

Remember that promise that God made to Abraham all those years earlier? We are about to watch how God is going to be faithful to fulfill *His Promise*. Ultimately, that is what the promise to Joseph is really about. What he sees at the beginning when he has the dream is him. I'm sure at some level he was convinced and believed that the promise wasn't just *for* him, but it was also *about* him. But for Joseph, and for you and I, the promise for our lives is never disconnected from God's bigger Promise and plan.

> # THE PROMISE FOR OUR LIVES IS NEVER DISCONNECTED FROM GOD'S BIGGER PROMISE AND PLAN.

Too often, I believe that we are more than willing to embrace the idea of the promise and all the benefits that we see coming along with it. For Joseph what he originally saw was his brothers and his mother and father bowing down to him. In other words, he was going to be kind of a big deal. But that wasn't really what the *promise* was about. We must avoid the mistake of embracing the idea of the *promise* without also embracing the reality of the process that God is going to use to prepare us to live out the promise.

> # WE MUST AVOID THE MISTAKE OF EMBRACING THE IDEA OF THE *PROMISE* WITHOUT ALSO EMBRACING THE REALITY OF THE PROCESS THAT GOD IS GOING TO USE TO PREPARE US TO LIVE OUT THE PROMISE.

So, what is your rocket ship? What is that promise, that call, that dream that you feel like God has given you? Have you given up on it? Do you feel like it will never happen? Have you convinced yourself that you are disqualified, that God has forgotten about you, that you have hit a dead end and there is no room to turn around? Maybe it is time for you to pull out the paper and the crayons again and consider the *promise*. It could be that the dream isn't over. Instead, maybe you are right in the middle of the process that is preparing you to take hold of the promise.

In order for Joseph to get to the promise there was going to be a process that would prepare him. Maybe that is where we are at in the journey as well.

Next stop along the journey for Joseph was a stop that he wasn't expecting. I don't think any of us ever expect the pit.

Chapter 3: **The PIT**

It wasn't supposed to go like this...

I'm an idealist. I will be the first to admit it. If a meeting is going to take me 20 minutes to drive to, I am convinced because Jesus loves me and because of my superior driving skills, it will only require me 16 minutes. This means that I have 4 additional minutes to get something else accomplished. Idealism can be a fun world to live in. The cup is always half full. Things are stacked in your favor. Everything is going to work out just like I have been planning. There is only one small problem that arises every so often: *reality*.

A little over two years ago we started the journey of becoming foster parents. After a few months of praying, talking and training, we received our first child into our home. He was five days old. Our entire family was filled with so much love and joy at his arrival. One morning, Amber had an early meeting, which meant that I had to make sure that all four kids were dressed, fed, lunches packed and ready for the day. I was confident in my abilities because we had already navigated this routine with our own three children. "How much harder can it be with one more?" I thought to myself.

I was ready for the day and we were making great progress to be out the door, just in time to get the big kids off to school. Then it happened. The new addition decided to test my diaper changing abilities. "No problem", I thought to myself, "I am a pro at this." As I laid him on the changing table, I checked the time. I had just enough to change him, get in the car and still make it on time. It was almost like he knew my thoughts and wanted to bring a touch of reality to me in that moment. As I was mid diaper change he did the unthinkable. Needless to say, that was not in the idealistically budgeted time to get to where we needed to go. We ended up late, very late that day because of circumstances beyond my control and realities that I wasn't expecting.

After Joseph's dream the story takes a somewhat unexpected shift. This young man who has experienced favor from his dad and now incredible dreams about his future would face the unexpected. No one ever signs up for unexpected moments, after all, they are *unexpected*. In the middle of these moments so many questions can begin to rise up. Before we get there, lets take a look at the first unexpected stop in Joseph's journey.

> "*When Joseph's brothers saw him coming, they recognized him in the distance. As he approached,* **they made plans to kill him. "Here comes the dreamer!"** *they said. "Come on, let's kill him and throw him into one of these cisterns. We can tell our father, 'A wild animal has eaten him.' Then we'll see what becomes of his dreams!" But when Reuben heard of their scheme, he came to Joseph's rescue. "Let's not kill him," he said. "Why should we shed any blood?* **Let's just throw him into this empty cistern here in the wilderness.** *Then he'll die without our laying a hand on him." Reuben was secretly planning to rescue Joseph and return him to his father.*" (Genesis 37:18–22, NLT)

Life brings challenges that we were not expecting. And sometimes those challenges can look an awful lot like a *pit*. Joseph's brothers want to see this little brother of theirs gone from the face of the earth. They start to plan it out. You can almost picture the eleven older brothers one-upping each other's ideas about what they are going to do with this problem they called Joseph. One of his brothers named Ruben didn't want to see this happen. I have a hunch that later on in life, Ruben became Joseph's favorite brother, but it's just a guess. Instead of killing young Joseph, they decide to throw him into a dried-up cistern – a pit. I can only imagine the shock and confusion running through Joseph's mind as he greets his brothers one moment, and then the next he is being tackled, attacked, stripped of his robe and then landing at the bottom of a deep, dark pit. Could he overhear them talking? Did he know what they were planning next? Did he see a way out? Did he know that God was going to use this?

We don't have the luxury of knowing everything that was going through his mind as he sat at the bottom of that pit, thinking and waiting. He had no control. He was completely at the mercy of his brothers. And from that vantage point, things are not looking good. But here is the good news for Joseph, and the good news for you and me: God is with us in the pit.

GOD IS WITH US IN THE PIT.

I had mentioned earlier that in jr. high I felt called by Jesus to become a youth pastor. It was my version of the dream that Joseph had. Over the next few years, I would aim my life in that direction, taking every step I knew to take that would get me to the destination. After graduating high school I started college at Northwest College (now Northwest University) in Kirkland, Washington. I was so thrilled to be taking steps to learn, grow and prepare to become a pastor and spend my life serving Jesus by serving others through the local church. Things, for the most part, were going exactly as I had planned and exactly as I thought they would.

I was doing well in my grades. I was loving the subjects that I was studying. My freshman year I had plugged in to a great local church in Issaquah, WA called Eastridge Church and I was getting opportunities to learn and grow under great pastors, leaders and mentors. Things were moving along and I could see how all of this was working together, just like I thought the plan should go. The summer after my sophomore year of college I traveled for the school with three other guys. We were on a ministry team together and spent the entire summer traveling to camps and churches. For me, there didn't seem to be a worry in the world because everything was going according to how I had planned it.

Fall hit and I began my junior year at Northwest. One weekend I had driven home to see my parents and my mom commented that I looked skinny. She asked if I was eating enough. What type of question is that for a guy in college? I reassured her that I was as I asked for more to drink. Later that fall, we spent Thanksgiving with my uncle and aunt and their family in Yakima. They commented that I was looking skinny too, but I reassured them I was fine and that it was probably just the types of food that I was eating. I remember that Thanksgiving feeling like I could never get over my thirst. I was always drinking something, trying to quench it. A few weeks later my mom convinced me to go see the doctor.

When I went in that day, I explained to him that I had lost some weight, but I felt just fine. Over the past few months I had gone from weighing 165 pounds down to 140. I was still doing great in school, serving at the church, and parking cars for a valet company on Lake Washington for a part time job. "It's probably nothing", he said, "But let's do a blood draw just in case." A number of days went by and I didn't really think much of it.

One afternoon I was working another one of my part time jobs, doing construction for my friend John. Three of us were out pressure washing for a client when John called and said we needed to return back to his house immediately. We were puzzled by the urgency in his request, but we packed everything up and drove back to his place in North Bend. I'll never forget the look on his face as I walked through his front door. "Tyler, I just got a call from your parents. The doctor contacted them with the results of the blood test you had done. They are driving up to get you right now and take you to the hospital. You have diabetes."

What?

I remember looking at him and saying "There's no way. I was *just* working a few minutes ago. I'm not sick…I am fine!" A few hours later I was sitting in a doctor's office. They had just checked my blood glucose and it was over 500. The doctor looked at me and said, "If there are ketones in your urine, you will be hospitalized immediately." I couldn't wrap my head around what was going on. A few hours ago, I was eating my lunch, working, and laughing with my co-workers and now I am being told that I might need to be hospitalized. This was *not* in the plan.

The next thing was the craziest part of that day. Some would think it was being told that you have Type 1 Diabetes. Nope. Next, the doctor handed me a syringe with insulin. As I'm now holding a needle I look at her and say, "What do you want me to do with *this*?" Clearly, she didn't know that I didn't "do" needles. So I explained that to her with great clarity and conviction. The doctor looked at me and smiled and with as much grace and certainty that she could give she simply said, "You do now. And you will for the rest of your life."

This was not a part of the plan. It wasn't supposed to happen like this. For a short moment, I felt like I was sitting at the bottom of a pit looking up, trying to figure out what just happened. This was a *pit* moment. I remember praying and asking God how this was supposed to work into His plan for my life. I tried my best to make sense out of all of this. I had moments where conversations with Jesus would go a little like this:

"I gave my life to you. You called me to give my life through serving you. I've done all of that. So why is *this* happening?"

I am thankful that God isn't scared of the questions we ask from the pit. He is big enough to handle our questions. Here's why: He can always see what we can't. In the moments that we can't figure out how this works into our plan or even His plan, He sees. He knows. And most important, He is with us in the pit.

WHERE DO I GO FROM HERE?

As Joseph is in the pit, I wonder what questions he was asking. When you have nothing but a pit, it seems like asking questions is probably a good way to pass this time. My guess is at some level he thought about what was next. How could he possibly get out of this? And if he does, how will they get past the awkwardness at family dinner next week? He probably wondered if this would be his last stop. But what he soon finds out is that the pit isn't permanent.

THE PIT ISN'T PERMANENT.

Although we would never willingly choose a pit moment, they have an ability to develop something inside of us. Trust. Joseph in his own power could do nothing to change or transform this situation that he found himself in. When I received by diagnosis in early 2001, there was nothing I could do to change that situation. It provided an environment for trust to be developed in my life.

What about your pit? What is it that God is wanting to cultivate in you through this stop along the journey? Here is a secret about the pits that we face

47

in our lives: the pits are playing a process in preparing us. Joseph didn't see it in the moment. His brothers definitely didn't see it. But while God was with him in the pit, He was beginning to cultivate this young man for something great! But soon there would be another unexpected turn: he was about to be sold by his brothers.

> "*Then, just as they were sitting down to eat, they looked up and saw a caravan of camels in the distance coming toward them. It was a group of Ishmaelite traders taking a load of gum, balm, and aromatic resin from Gilead down to Egypt. Judah said to his brothers, "**What will we gain** by killing our brother? We'd have to cover up the crime. Instead of hurting him, **let's sell him** to those Ishmaelite traders. After all, he is our brother—our own flesh and blood!" And his brothers agreed. So when the Ishmaelites, who were Midianite traders, came by, Joseph's brothers pulled him out of the cistern and sold him to them for twenty pieces of silver. And the traders took him to Egypt.*" (Genesis 37:25–28, NLT)

Imagine what it must have felt like when the rope was thrown down to him in the bottom of the pit. I'm sure he was thinking that he was glad this prank was over! He couldn't wait for time to pass so that they could all look back at this and laugh about it down the road. But as he is being pulled out, Joseph realizes that he is moving from one *pit* to another: now he is going to be sold as a slave. To add more pain to the situation, his own brothers are going to profit from this incredibly painful moment. There are multiple reasons why the pit moments of life can be painful. And if we are not careful, there are subtle lies that we can begin to believe about the pit. Let's look at a few of them and how Jesus is actually able to use our pit moments for our good and His glory.

PAIN FROM THE PIT

Pain is never at the top of our request list. As I said earlier, we often do everything we can to avoid pain. When we face moments of pain, the temptation is to believe that God is giving us this pain because we did something to deserve it, maybe He is mad at us and we are getting payback for our poor choices or that He just dishes out whatever He feels like on a given day. But all of these thoughts neglect to take in the true character and nature of who God is. If you want to know what God is like, look at Jesus! Scripture teaches us that Jesus is the *visible* image of the *invisible* God (Colossians 1:15). Jesus met people in their pain. He brought freedom and healing. He said He came to set captives free. So, when you find yourself in a pit moment, and its painful you can begin to believe a few things that, even though they sound right, are not.

Here are a few lies to reject about the pit.

LIE #1:

THE PIT IS PUNISHMENT

This is a common lie that so many people buy in to. They believe that when things go wrong in life, when unexpected moments of pain show up, that somehow that is God's method of payment for all that you have done wrong. I do believe that our choices *can* lead to encountering pits. At times we can make decisions and choices that dig the pit for ourselves. But if God had a payback system of pits and pain for you and I, there was no need to send Jesus as our rescuer. Scripture teaches us that the punishment that we deserved, Jesus carried for us (Isaiah 53:4-6). Instead of seeing punishment in the pit, look for purpose.

LIE #2:

THE PROMISE MUST NOT BE REAL

Some of us choose to believe that when we encounter a challenge like a pit, that the dream or the promise we were pursuing must not have been real. We tell ourselves that if God really promised this to me, then I shouldn't have to go through this. But just like Joseph, the promise was and is real. Just because you face a pit it doesn't mean that God has abandon or forgotten His promise.

LIE #3:

I AM ALONE IN THIS PIT

Joseph, through this pit will learn that he is not alone, nor will he ever be. As I had to process the reality of being diagnosed with Type 1 Diabetes, I learned that I was not alone in navigating this in my life. God was with me. And no matter how dark that pit might look right now, you are not alone.

LIE #4:

IF GOD WAS GOOD, I WOULDN'T BE *IN* THIS PIT

This lie is a dangerous one to believe. Whenever we experience pain, confusion, loss or conflict we know that it doesn't *feel* good. And we all like to feel good. It is important to understand that God is good, even when life doesn't feel good. We need to remind ourselves often that God doesn't just "do" good, He *is* good! It is His nature. When we have a pit season, it doesn't mean that God is no longer good. It simply can mean that we have a good God with us as we navigate this pit. We have a good God with us who is taking what we might consider a setback and working it for our good and His glory.

When I sat in that doctors office I was tempted to question God's goodness. I had been serving Him for years. I wanted to dwell on this question: "If He is good, why did this happen to me?" But I began to learn that if I only accept what I see as good, what does that say about my trust? No, I don't believe that God "gave" me diabetes. I believe that my pancreas decided to stop working. He has grown me in ways through navigating my health that I don't know would have happened. Doors have opened up for me to talk with students and other individuals who are living every day, dependent on insulin. You see, my pit not only was preparing me, it is also connecting me with others.

We must remember that nothing is wasted in God's economy! Nothing. So maybe you thought there would be no pits along the journey. Maybe as you navigate a challenge or pain right now in your life, you question God's wisdom or even His presence. You are wondering how on earth this is actually going to get you any closer to where you feel He has called you to go. Remember, nothing is wasted.

NOTHING IS WASTED.

Joseph had some time in the pit, and now he has been sold as a slave and is in route to Egypt. The next stop on Joseph's journey was a place called Potiphar's house. The process of preparation wasn't done yet. Little did he know the pressure that he was about to encounter, and the price tag that sometimes comes along with making the *right* decisions.

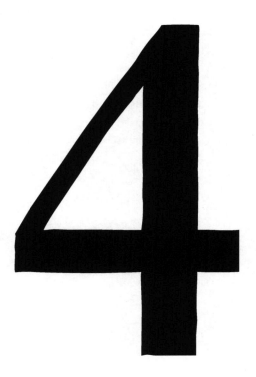

Chapter 4: **The PRESSURE**

When trouble comes, and you didn't even go looking for it.

I remember my 6th grade very well. I was just starting to get into skateboarding and rock music. I finally gained access to something other than the Carmen or Psalty's Praise cassette tapes that my parents got me at the local Christian book store. For me, life felt like it was good. Because I went to a local school that had recently adapted an intermediate model of school, I still had at least one recess every day. What can be better than that? 6th grade *AND* recess! But during that year, some things started to change. For one, my skin on my face started to develop these dots and spots. My mom told me they were called pimples. Another thing started happening in that time period: people who I thought were my friends, I quickly found out that they were something else.

One specific day that is still etched into my mind involved an interaction with a kid in my class named Sam. Sam and I had been buddies – not best friends, but we got along. He was good at soccer, and I was good at swings. Yes, you read that right – the best asset I brought to the playground in those days was my ability to do backflips off of the swings. Maybe *that* was my problem right there? One day, Sam thought it would be funny to begin to point out the "chickenpox looking things" on my face. At first, I tried to brush it off and just told Sam to shut up. But he persisted. Soon, another friend caught on to what Sam was doing and started laughing. Before I knew it, it felt like the whole class was looking, pointing and laughing. The rest of the day, walking through the hall, it seemed like everyone was looking at my face and the spots on it. For the next few days it became the joke.

A few days later, while in line, the joking started again. I had finally reached my breaking point. This wasn't okay. This wasn't right. What did I do to deserve this? *So, I decided to fight back.* I shoved Sam against the wall. He immediately pushed me back and soon, we were face to face about to swing at each other when our teacher intervened. I found myself asking,

"Why is this happening?"

"What can I do about this?"

"This doesn't seem *fair…*"

For those who have ever faced a time in life where you faced some trouble, even when you didn't go looking for it – our friend Joseph can relate. After Joseph's encounter with the pit, he found himself as a captive to the Ishmaelites headed to Egypt to be sold as a slave. I wonder what his teenage mind was thinking about this part of the journey. This didn't feel much like the promise that he had seen in his dreams. Upon arriving in Egypt, he was placed up on the trading block. Soon, a wealthy ruler in Egypt named Potiphar took notice of Joseph. Joseph was sold as property to Potiphar, to work as a slave in his household.

No matter how nice that house was, there is no way that Joseph was thinking this was the destination of the promise. Nice rooms, marble floors, beautiful gardens – but not the palace. Even though this was one more unexpected turn for Joseph, God was with him and in His grace, God was using this part of Joseph's story to prepare him for the promise. Not only that, but even in the midst of this chapter of his life, God was giving Joseph *favor*.

> *"When Joseph was taken to Egypt by the Ishmaelite traders, he was purchased by Potiphar, an Egyptian officer. Potiphar was captain of the guard for Pharaoh, the king of Egypt.* **The LORD was with Joseph,** *so he succeeded in everything he did as he served in the home of his Egyptian master.* **Potiphar noticed this and realized that the LORD was with Joseph, giving him success in everything he did.** *This pleased Potiphar, so he soon made Joseph his personal attendant. He put him in charge of his entire household and everything he owned. From the day Joseph was put in charge of his master's household and property,* **the LORD began to bless Potiphar's household for Joseph's sake.** *All his household affairs ran smoothly, and his crops and livestock flourished. So Potiphar gave Joseph complete administrative responsibility over everything he owned. With Joseph there, he didn't worry about a thing—except what kind of food to eat!*
>
> (Genesis 39:1–6, NLT)

FAVOR IN UNEXPECTED PLACES

Since the day that Joseph had his God-given dream, it seems as if things are continually moving *away* from its fulfillment, not toward it. The Pit was bad enough, but now to spend his days serving as a slave in Potiphar's house? How does this work into the plan? If you have ever asked yourself a similar question when navigating unexpected seasons, I want you to notice something important that scripture says about this moment in Josephs life: *"The Lord was with Joseph…"*

That statement alone makes all of the difference. We can find ourselves in the most unexpected, painful or discouraging situations – but if the Lord is with us, favor can show up in unexpected places. God was allowing this moment to be one more piece of the cultivation process that Joseph would need for his future. Joseph was experiencing success. Everything he managed *got better*. Often in life, we only improve the things that we want to improve. Joseph, serving as a slave, improved everything that was given to him to manage and his master Potiphar took notice. It was through this that Joseph was elevated to the place of becoming the personal assistant to Potiphar and was tasked with overseeing everything on the property and the household. God was bringing favor in unexpected places.

If all of this wasn't enough, God added his blessing to Potiphar's home. And catch this: it wasn't for *Potiphar's* sake, it was for *Joseph's* sake! How cool is that? Here is this young teenage boy who has been taken from his homeland against his will, sold into slavery and God is bringing him *favor in unexpected places*. That is grace. It seems like things couldn't get any better for young Joseph. He has a new job description. He is over everyone in the household, developing his management and leadership gifts. I wonder if he is beginning to think, *"Maybe this is the palace?"* Maybe this is the place where everything is going to turn around? But little did he know the pressure he was about to experience and the price tag that would accompany being faithful.

UNDER PRESSURE

Some of us thrive under pressure. When we get our backs up against the wall and everything is at stake, somehow, we find a whole different gear to operate with. Others tend to completely shut down when the heat gets turned up and the pressure is on. Which one are you? I believe it is important to know how you react and respond, because it isn't a matter of *if* you experience a moment of pressure – it is a matter of *when* you will face pressure. And when the pressure is on, how we respond makes all of the difference.

At some level, it appears like things are moving in the right direction for Joseph. There was one problem: he was good looking. I know that is an idea that most of us wouldn't consider a problem. But for Joseph, a little less beauty or a few less abs on the six-pack could have helped him potentially avoid a run-in with a high-pressure situation. Because of his looks, he caught the attention of the *wrong person*: Potiphar's wife.

> "...Joseph was a very handsome and well-built young man, and Potiphar's wife soon began to look at him lustfully. "Come and sleep with me," she demanded. But Joseph refused. "Look," he told her, "my master trusts me with everything in his entire household. No one here has more authority than I do. He has held back nothing from me except you, because you are his wife. How could I do such a wicked thing? It would be a great sin against God." **She kept putting pressure on Joseph day after day,** but he refused to sleep with her, and he kept out of her way as much as possible."
>
> (Genesis 39:6–10, NLT)

I'm not sure how you define pressure, but if you are young, away from home, you've been betrayed by your family, and a rich woman is taking notice of you – it seems like a perfect recipe for pressure. It is one thing to face pressure when most of the circumstances are going good in life. Pressure feels different when you have been on top of reading the Bible, your prayer life is great, your marriage has never been stronger, you're getting enough sleep, you have been eating right and exercising consistently. But have you noticed how pressure feels different when things are out of alignment? Have you noticed how things that wouldn't usually catch your attention do? Thoughts that you would normally throw aside, all of the sudden seem to take up residence without even asking permission. Desires that wouldn't even seem enticing now feel like they have you in their gravitational pull.

For our young friend, his struggle against pressure is real. I think at times it is easy to isolate people we read about in scripture and pretend like they somehow got a pass from facing things like we face. At times we can read and convince ourselves that it must have been easier in their shoes because God must have given them a heavenly bypass to experiencing the tug and pull of their humanity. But this simply is not true. Young Joseph had every emotion and hormone that every other individual has. The pain he experienced was real. The rejection he experienced was real. The loneliness that he navigated was real. The betrayal, the isolation, the distance, the fact that he was sold by his brothers and is alone in a foreign land – all of these things are very real.

If you are facing pressure, it is important to remember that it isn't because you have necessarily done something wrong. Obviously, we can sometimes cause our own pressure points through making decisions that were not the best. Joseph reminds us, however, that you can be doing your best in life, in work and even in honoring God and you may still experience pressure.

Pressure doesn't make exceptions. No matter who you are, where you are from, how much money you make, how well known you are or how spiritually mature you are – you are guaranteed to experience *pressure*. What I love about this moment in Joseph's life is that the pressure does something important. As we watch him engage with the pressure it accomplishes something in him that it does for each of us as well.

PRESSURE REVEALS WHAT IS ON THE INSIDE.

In the moment of his pressure with Potiphar's wife, we get a front row seat to see what is actually on the inside in Joseph's life. His response to this pressure is incredibly important:

> *"...How could I do such a wicked thing? It would be a great sin against God.'"* (Genesis 39:9 NLT)

Do you see it? Did you notice that in the greatest moment of pressure, what actually came out of Joseph?

It wasn't a focus on himself.

It wasn't that he was concerned with what his master Potiphar might say or think.

He wasn't worried about how this decision might impact his social media following.

Joseph was focused on how this would impact his relationship with his God.

If we wait until we are in the middle of the pressure to decided what our priorities will actually be, we are too late. None of us do our best life values development when the pressure is on. Our values are cultivated over time — not in the heat of the moment. What we are learning through the life of Joseph is that he had a value system that was intact *before* the pressure hit. He had already determined at some point that he would filter his decisions, even decisions that are under pressure, with an internal value system. For young Joseph, the primary filter was his relationship with God.

When we encounter the pressure points, how often is that our *actual* filter? Let me be clear: all of us use some type of filter to make decisions. All that moments of pressure do is reveal what is on the inside.

THE PAIN OF DISCIPLINE IS EASIER THAN THE PAIN OF REGRET

When I was in jr. high I remember a leader in my life telling me that *"the pain of discipline is easier than the pain of regret."* Little did I know at that moment how true the idea actually is. How many times have you found yourself wishing you could rewind the tape and simply made the payment of self-discipline on the front end of the decision, than paying the heavy price of regret later on? Joseph made a disciplined decision.

He made a decision based on his goal. In addition to discipline, I think it is important to note that Joseph's decision was ultimately a *faith* decision. He had to trust that God had something better. He had to see what he couldn't see and be sure of what he was hoping for (Hebrews 11:1). Faith and discipline go hand in hand when it comes to making God-honoring decisions in the midst of the pressure.

DON'T GIVE UP WHAT YOU WANT MOST FOR WHAT YOU WANT IN THE MOMENT.

The mistake that many of us make is that we are willing to sacrifice what we want MOST for what is available in the MOMENT. The simple truth is that doing right and doing wrong both have a price tag. Every decision we make will cost us at some level. When the pressure is on, remember what you actually want *most*. Again, this needs to be decided before the pressure is on. Joseph had made this choice sometime before his encounter with Potiphar's wife.

What is it that you actually desire *most*? All of us has something that falls into this category. Each of us are driven by a desire or a dream that is an ultimate pursuit. Maybe for you it is comfort, a relationship, financial security, the desire to be loved or known, excelling in a career, breaking a record in sports or some other achievement…the list could go on and on. Figuring this out is an important step, because when we get clarity on what we want most it helps to shape our choices and decisions. I encourage you to take some time toward the close of this chapter to reflect, think and ask yourself: what is it that I want most in life? When the pressure is on, it will be revealed.

One final note on this stop on our journey with Joseph. Losing your *coat* is better than losing your *character*. Joseph reminds us that sometimes the best plan is to run away from the pressure, not worrying about what we are leaving behind.

LOSING YOUR *COAT* IS BETTER THAN LOSING YOUR *CHARACTER*.

I wonder how many times the pressure has left scars simply because we tried to hang on too long. We need to be willing to ask the Holy Spirit for wisdom to discern the moments when it is best for us to stand our ground and when it is maybe best for us to leave our coat and run.

This is the second time that Joseph has lost a coat that was significant to him. The coat his father gave him all those years ago that represented his favor was stripped from him before the pit. This coat, that more than likely represented his status in the household of Potiphar was now stripped from him before his journey to the prison. If I am Joseph, at this point I am thinking to myself, "Maybe I should just give up on the idea of having special coats moving forward." But in the not too distant future, he will receive another coat.

Before we get there, however, Joseph has a little detour to a place called *Prison*.

</a

Chapter 5: **The PRISION**

Waiting for freedom and feeling forgotten

Have you ever done the *right* thing, and still ended up in what you thought was the *wrong* place? A few years ago, my sister and brother-in-law and their family were home from Africa where they serve as missionaries. Over Christmas, we decided to get all of our families together and rented a cabin up in the mountains. The plan was to take a few days away, playing in the snow and creating fun family memories. When we arrived there was a good amount of snow. Amber and I had a car with all-wheel drive, so we were not too concerned. A few hours later, we knew the rest of the family would be arriving, so I decided to pull our car to the side of the drive way to make space for the other cars that were coming to the cabin. As I began to pull the car to the side of the driveway, I pulled on to what I thought was a patch of untouched snow. What I didn't realize is there was nothing *under* the snow but a foot of air. Before I knew it, my car was high centered on the snow and I couldn't get enough traction to get the car unstuck. It had looked like a good plan and had felt like the right thing to do. For the next few hours I was busy digging out the car, practicing the fruit of patience and working to get it back up onto the driveway. I wanted to do the right thing, and it ended up creating a frustrating situation.

What's the moral of the story?

All-wheel drive works best when there is ground to drive on.

Joseph faced *Pressure* from Potiphar's wife as we talked about in the previous chapter. He did the right thing, choosing to not forfeit what he wanted most: to honor God. Because of the rejection Potiphar's wife had received, she lied to her husband and had Joseph thrown into prison. Again, we look at the circumstances and feel like our friend can't seem to catch a break. But as we step back, we see how God is using the *process* that Joseph is going through to *prepare* him.

"Potiphar was furious when he heard his wife's story about how Joseph had treated her. So he took Joseph and threw him into the prison where the king's prisoners were held, and there he remained. **But the LORD was with Joseph in the prison and showed him his faithful love.** *And the LORD made Joseph a favorite with the prison warden. Before long, the warden put Joseph in charge of all the other prisoners and over everything that happened in the prison. The warden had no more worries, because Joseph took care of everything. The LORD was with him and caused everything he did to succeed."* (Genesis 39:19–23, NLT)

No doubt, this prison felt like a massive disconnect from the dream that Joseph had received when he was 17 and wearing the beautiful coat his father had given him. It is hard to imagine all that is going through Joseph's head. Over the past season he has had to navigate betrayal, rejection, abandonment, loneliness and false accusations. He is in a new culture with new cultural, social and religious norms. To top all of this off, he is now in the king's prison.

The dream that Joseph had years before didn't include prison, yet in His grace, God was protecting, preserving and preparing Joseph to be in the right place at the right time. We have all heard the idea that hindsight is 20/20. My guess is if you were to take some time and look through the journey of your life, there were moments that you thought maybe God had forgotten about you or somehow *He* made a mistake. In the moment, those emotions and feelings are *real* – they just aren't *true*. Just like God hadn't forgotten about Joseph, He hasn't forgotten about you.

If you look back over those moments where you felt alone, you may begin to see in a new way how God was actually using the moment to prepare you for something even greater. What looked like a prison was just one more stop in the process.

WANTING FREEDOM AND FEELING FORGOTTEN

Have you realized the difference between God's timing and your timing? If you are anything like me, I am convinced that God's schedule should be in perfect agreement with my schedule and to-do list. Yet, the longer that I have followed Jesus the more I realize it isn't God's schedule that is messed up. It is mine.

When this happens in our lives you can quickly convince yourself that somehow God has forgotten you. You want to get out of the prison that you find yourself in. You long for *freedom* but you feel *forgotten*. I'm confident that Joseph felt forgotten in his time in the prison. In Genesis 40:1 it says, "Some time later...". We are not exactly sure how much time has passed, but any amount of time in prison, especially when it wasn't on your goal sheet for the year, is going to feel far too long.

Have you ever felt like God has forgotten about you? Have you ever felt forgotten by others? It is easy to see how Joseph could have felt both overlooked and forgotten by God and the people who said they would remember. Take a few minutes to read through Genesis chapter 40. Joseph is in prison and time keeps passing. Soon, he is joined by a few of Pharaoh's servants: a cupbearer and the chief baker. The captain who was in charge of the prison placed these men under Joseph's care. Time continues to pass and then one night both the cupbearer and the chief baker have dreams.

As Joseph sees them the next day he can tell that they are concerned. After questioning them and finding out that they both had dreams on the same night, Joseph tells them that God is able to interpret their dreams for them. Joseph doesn't see it yet, but God is connecting all of the dots to get him in the right place at the right time. Even in the prison, God is preparing Joseph.

He was preparing Joseph's administrative gifts as he oversees the operations of the prison.

He was preparing Joseph's ability to listen and discern.

He was preparing Joseph's character and capacity so that he could shoulder the responsibility that came along with the fulfillment of the promise.

God was at work, even within the prison. If Joseph hadn't been in the prison when Pharaoh's attendants were placed there, who would have helped them understand the meaning of the dreams? As Joseph interprets the dreams for them, one is favorable and one isn't. One man is restored to his position and one is put to death. As the cupbearer is headed out to his restored position, Joseph asks him a favor: *"And **please remember me** and do me a favor when things go well for you. Mention me to Pharaoh, **so he might let me out of this place.**" (Genesis 40:14)*

Even though young Joseph makes this heart-felt plea, he was soon forgotten by the cupbearer. He was forgotten by the person he helped but he was not forgotten by God. He had hoped that Pharaoh would get him out, not realizing that God already had a plan for his release…and God's plan was much bigger than just getting out of prison. God's plan went beyond what Joseph could begin to imagine.

GOD *SEES YOU* AND HE IS *WITH YOU.*

It is vital that you understand a radically important truth: *You are not forgotten.* Even if all seems lost and hopeless, God *sees you* and He is *with you.* Joseph wasn't yet free from the prison, but freedom was on its way. His time of waiting in the prison wasn't wasted. Here are some lessons that we can learn from Joseph's stop in the prison.

Lesson #1:

NOTHING IS WASTED IN GOD'S ECONOMY.

If you find yourself in a "prison" season, it is critical that you remind yourself of this important fact: God doesn't waste *anything.* This can be hard to come to terms with. I have had many moments where I have wrestled with God about what I have walked through. Some things we face in life seem pointless and a waste. When we choose to look through a different lens and understand that He is actually "working *all things* together" for good (Romans 8:28), we can see with new clarity that places of pain, disappointment or even prison moments are being used for His purpose. Be confident in this truth: God is at work for your good and His glory!

You may be confused by those moments when you did the right thing, and it feels like you still lost. In those places and spaces, remind yourself of this lesson: *nothing* is wasted. God is at work. I am not forgotten. He will use *this*.

Sounds crazy, right? How can we possibly look at the messes and things we look at as wasted moments and think that anything good can come from it. But here is a beautifully simple truth: Jesus has a way of taking what we see as problems and making them into probabilities. This is a gift. Sure, it may not feel like it in the moment, but in His economy – absolutely nothing is wasted!

Lesson #2:

NOT EVERY PRISON HAS BARS.

Even though Joseph may have been *in* prison, *prison* wasn't in him. He found a way to thrive in the place that he was. The truth is that I have met many people throughout the years who have never been to prison, jail or even experienced house arrest. But they are caged. They are trapped. They are confined. I learned a long time ago that some people live in a prison without even knowing it. They can't see it because there are no physical bars – yet the impact is the same.

Joseph thrived in unexpected places. What about you? Are you in prison with your thoughts, your habits, your anger or your past? We must remember that Jesus came to set captives free (Luke 4:18). We must embrace the truth that He desires us to walk in freedom. We see in the life of Joseph, as well as others throughout the pages of scripture (like the Apostle Paul) that you can be chained up, yet still be *free*. You don't need bars to be in prison, and a lack of bars doesn't mean that you're free.

Prison can be a stop along the journey or it can be a state of mind. We choose. You may not see bars in front of you, but the vital question is do you live like they are there?

Maybe you have heard of how circuses train elephants to not run away? When they are young, they tie a rope around their leg and stake it to the ground so that they can't move beyond the length of the rope. It becomes their prison. At a young age, they are trained and conditioned to respond to the reality that they can't move beyond the limit of the length of the rope and the strength of the stake in the ground. As they grow older, the mindset is so engrained and trained within them that they will never move beyond it. *It is a prison without bars.* What would only take a fraction of their strength to snap the rope or lift the stake from the ground never happens – the prison is too real for them to do anything else.

Are you in a prison without bars? Allow Jesus to transform your mind about the circumstances you find yourself in today. You may be in a prison moment, but the prison doesn't have to be in you!

Lesson #3:

GOD IS STILL WITH YOU.

I love that we are reminded this powerful truth about Joseph's time in prison: God was *with* Him. We know this by the way God used him to miraculously interpret dreams while behind bars. But we see God's presence with Joseph in other ways too.

God positioned Joseph with growth opportunities even while in prison. He was placed in charge – no doubt a highly administrative role. This is going to come in handy in the days ahead. Instead of administrating a prison, God was preparing him to administrate a nation and the plan to save many from starvation. What you may see as unimportant in the assignment that you currently have could be critical for the plan that God has for you and others in the days ahead.

It is clear that God never lost sight or interest in Joseph. This young man was going to play a critical role in the advancement of God's rescue plan for mankind. God knew where he was and what he needed. Being all knowing, God also saw how the timing was going to play out. Doesn't this bring you comfort? I love that God is not only aware of us but He is also *with us*.

Don't allow your current circumstances to lie to you or rob you from this truth. I would encourage you to give Him space to remind you of this reality today. Don't wait. Don't put it off. Allow Jesus space to show up where you are at and within what you are currently navigating.

Lesson #4:

FAVOR FOLLOWS FAITHFULNESS – EVEN IN UNEXPECTED PLACES

The final lesson I want us to recognize from Joseph's time in the prison is that favor follows faithfulness – even in unexpected places. Prison is probably not on your top ten list for places where God is going to show incredible favor – but that is exactly what He does for Joseph. I love the statement we read earlier from Genesis 39, that God was with

Joseph in the prison and showed him His *faithful love*. To me, that is a great definition of favor.

God revealed His faithful love. It doesn't matter how dark the prison cell was: His faithful love was being revealed. When the loneliness of prison crept in, the faithful love of God pressed in harder. When memories of family betrayal and rejection flooded our young friend's mind, God's faithful love moved in to fill the void. God's love showed itself. This is the beautiful truth about how God reveals His love. It finds us. No matter how real the pain or "prison" may be, God's love presses in to where we are. Even as I write this, I've been reminded multiple times over this past year that God's faithfulness reveals itself in unexpected places and in unexpected ways. The moments that seem most painful become a meeting point between our reality and a greater reality: God's goodness, grace and faithfulness.

Many of us live with a picture of God's favor that isn't complete or accurate. Maybe we think that God's favor only shows up on a Sunday at a specific time and location. Maybe we are conditioned to think that favor can only be accessed because we dress right, act right or are in the right place. Joseph's stop in the prison screams something radically different to us.

God shows up with His favor in unexpected places. That favor followed Joseph's faithfulness. Let me be clear: Joseph didn't earn it. His faithfulness didn't force God's favor. Our actions never have the power to control or back God into a corner. The goal of our faithfulness should never be *leverage* – the goal should be *love*. I desire to be faithful because of His faithfulness to me. As Joseph walked in faithfulness to God, from the pit, through the pressure and in the prison – God's favor continued to follow him.

I hope that today, you find comfort in the fact that you are seen, you're not alone, and that even if you find yourself in a prison moment, God is with you and He hasn't forgotten the *Promise*.

Our friend Joseph is about to experience how committed to the *Promise* God is, and its about to become clear as he steps into the *Palace*.

Chapter 6: **The PALACE**

It wasn't just about me.

There is nothing quite like experiencing a dream come true, especially a dream that you have been holding on to for years. I still remember the day I got my drivers license. I had hoped and prayed for this moment for *years*. To be honest, I wasn't sure if it would ever happen. This was due to the fact that a constant topic at church and among friends was Jesus return and the Rapture. I know this might sound crazy to you, but I had legitimate concern about my dreams of getting my license since Jesus might come back before I had the chance. In my 11 year old mind, this was a big deal. I wanted Jesus to come and rapture His people – I just wanted to be able to drive first. One memory specifically sticks out to me when I was at my cousins house. I asked Jesus that if He was going to return could we please coordinate it after I had my drivers license...and maybe after I got married.

The day finally arrived and I passed the test. I had my license and the rapture still hadn't happened! The unfortunate thing is I didn't have my own car. As disappointing as this might have been, there was good news: my parents owned a nice full-sized white van. It was the kind of van in the mid 90's that was somewhat popular. It had a TV and a VCR (I had to describe what a VCR was to my children a few weeks back. They asked how you selected different chapters of the movie...I let them know there were two options: fast forward speed 1 and fast forward speed 2). Oh, the good old days! The night I got my license my parents let me take out the car – which was a full sized van – and go pick up my friend and drive around Tacoma. The laws of not having a passenger until you had logged enough months of driving didn't yet exist – so off we went into the early summer evening. The music was loud, the laughs were real and after years of waiting and praying the dream of having my license came true.

When we started with young Joseph, he had received a God-given dream. At 17 years old, he was certain that the dream was all about *him*. Remember his vantage point when he received the dreams? He was at the center and his family was bowing down to him. There was no way at 17 did he understand or comprehend the journey he would go on – the process that God would take him through – to see the fulfillment of the dream.

In the last chapter we talked about Joseph's time in prison. There is no way that Joseph ever had imagined that his life trajectory would take him to a place where he was wrongly accused and also forgotten about. Yet there he was, in the king's prison. How many times did he replay the dreams in his mind? How many times did he imagine what life *could have been*? The days bleed into weeks. The weeks bleed into months and the months to years.

Will I ever get out of this place?

Was the dream even real?

Then one day, everything changes.

> "***Two full years later***, *Pharaoh dreamed...*"
> (Genesis 41:1, NLT)

Pharaoh has a series of dreams that leaves him completely disturbed and troubled. He gathered around him his best and brightest, yet none could help him discover what the imagery meant from his dreams. Pharaoh has nowhere to look for clarity among his own people, until the cup-bearer speaks up.

> *"Finally, the king's chief cup-bearer spoke up. "Today I have been reminded of my failure," he told Pharaoh. "Some time ago, you were angry with the chief baker and me, and you imprisoned us in the palace of the captain of the guard. One night the chief baker and I each had a dream, and each dream had its own meaning.* **There was a young Hebrew man** *with us in the prison who was a slave of the captain of the guard.* **We told him our dreams, and he told us what each of our dreams meant. And everything happened just as he had predicted.** *I was restored to my position as cup-bearer, and the chief baker was executed and impaled on a pole."*
>
> *Pharaoh sent for Joseph at once, and he was quickly brought from the prison. After he shaved and changed his clothes, he went in and stood before Pharaoh. Then Pharaoh said to Joseph, "I had a dream last night, and no one here can tell me what it means.* **But I have heard that when you hear about a dream you can interpret it.**"" (Genesis 41:9–15, NLT)

What Joseph says next is shocking. He tells Pharaoh that *he can't* interpret his dreams.

Are you serious Joseph? This is your chance? You can take things into your own hands! This is your opportunity to get things in life back on track.

But Joseph had learned something important during his journey. Throughout the process that God was guiding him through he began to come to terms with a simple yet powerful truth: *I can't...But God can!* Joseph understood that there was going to be one Hero in this story and it wasn't going to be himself. God was going to get the credit. Only God had the ability to interpret this dream. And only God could take Joseph from the prison and bring him to the palace. It wasn't going to be Joseph's effort, skills, gifts, moral track record, social media following or leadership prowess. Joseph couldn't get himself to the palace. Joseph wasn't going to be the one who would fulfill God's promise. The part that Joseph would play is the part that you and I play – we trust God as He directs us and grows us through the process.

What happens next is amazing. Pharaoh is pleased by Joseph's God-given interpretation and plan. With famine coming, and a window of opportunity to be proactive and do something about it Pharaoh makes the decision to put Joseph as second in command over all of Egypt. Imagine that – a few minutes ago you were sitting in a jail cell feeling forgotten about and now you are second in command in one of the greatest kingdoms in the history of the world.

In addition to this you get that new top of the line chariot to ride in, Pharaohs signet ring and *new clothes* (Genesis 41:42-43). Don't miss that last part. It is easy to move past quickly and miss the significance. Do you remember how this journey with Joseph started? His dad gave him a robe – a special robe and it was stripped from him. At Potiphar's house Joseph had another robe ripped from him. Now, as this dream all these years in the making is coming to pass Joseph is given a *new robe*. Finally, he has a coat that won't be stripped from him!

How cool is that? So many things that had been lost and taken, God in His grace is restoring!

It would be easy at this point for some around Joseph to look at him and think, "He's just an overnight success." "Five minutes ago he was in prison, now look at him…" What we need to remember is what appeared to be an overnight success was actually 13 years in the making.

There were 13 years of learning, growing and trusting.

There were 13 years of pits, pressures and prisons.

There were 13 years of holding on to God's promise as he learned to grow through the process.

After 13 years, you wouldn't think it was likely for this young man to end up as second in command over Egypt. But that was God's plan and purpose for Joseph. None of this was coincidence. I believe that too often in life we allow the idea that "it was just a coincidence" to rob our awareness of the process that God was guiding us through.

THINK FOR A MOMENT ABOUT ALL THE PROBABILITIES THAT HAD TO HAPPEN FOR JOSEPH TO BECOME SECOND IN COMMAND IN EGYPT:

1. Jacob had to show favoritism to his son, Joseph
2. Joseph's brothers had to develop a great hatred towards him.
3. Joseph needed to be sold as a slave to a caravan heading to Egypt
4. Potiphar had to purchase Joseph and employ him in his household
5. Potiphar's wife had to take notice of Joseph specifically
6. Potiphar's wife had to accuse Joseph wrongly.
7. Joseph had to be sent to prison.
8. The keeper of the prison had to like Joseph and give him free access throughout the prison.

9. Pharaoh's butler and baker had to put in prison.
10. Joseph had to meet and be there the exact day they were both anxious about their dreams.
11. Joseph had to be able to interpret their dreams.
12. The butler had to remember the experience for two years.
13. The butler had to be present the day Pharaoh's dreams went unexplained.
14. Pharaoh had to be willing to bring a prisoner into his court to try to interpret his dreams.
15. Joseph had to receive the interpretations of Pharaoh's dreams from God.

What we see as just probabilities or a series of coincidences could be God orchestrating a process to bring us to a place that we could never get to in our own strength, wisdom or ability.

> # HAVE YOU EVER CONSIDERED ALL THE MIRACLES THAT HAD TO TAKE PLACE TO GET YOU WHERE YOU ARE TODAY?

Take a moment right now to pause and reflect. What are all the places you could have ended up? Where are the moments that you were sure God had forgotten, but it was actually protecting and preserving you for where you are now? In all the probabilities, God had a plan! He was and is bringing you through a process.

One thing that strikes me about Joseph at this point is his humility. *"I can't…, but God can…"(Genesis 41:16)*. For Joseph, humility paved the way to honor. He wasn't weak or insecure. There was a powerful mixture of confidence with humility. Where does this type of confidence come from in our lives? I believe it is rooted in understanding that God is able. That is our confidence. And with this being true, this is also the key to walking in humility: it isn't about us. Humility in our lives happen when we recognize that *we are not the source*. Joseph couldn't, but he had a confidence that God could! No matter where you may be in your journey remember your source of confidence: God can! Remember you are not alone, nor is it a coincidence where God is guiding you in your process.

THE PROMISE MAY BE FOR ME BUT IT'S NOT ONLY ABOUT ME

It's not long after Joseph gives the interpretation of the dreams that he understands what the purpose of the dreams was *really* about all along. When he had the dreams at 17 years old, he thought it was about people bowing to him. Now, as he steps into the palace he realizes that the dream was about the salvation and the protection of people. God needed the right person, in the right place at the right time. Joseph was His guy for the job. The position wasn't about *him*. It was about *others*.

THE POSITION WAS ABOUT PEOPLE

The palace wasn't about Joseph. It wasn't about *his* comfort, *his* enjoyment or *his* popularity. This is one thing that is so quickly lost in our culture. So often when we think about position or opportunity, we think it is for us and about us. Years before, the fulfillment of this dream represented people bowing down to him. Now, years later he realized that God has positioned him where he is at to serve God by serving others. Joseph finally comes to a significant realization that I believe every Jesus follower should recognize: *It was about the rescue and salvation of* **others.**

No matter your job, role, position or title in life I believe that God has placed us where we are to partner with Him in His great rescue plan. You are in that job with a purpose. That campus that you attend every day has a cause. The children you are raising goes beyond the day to day tasks that fill your schedule. If you are a follower of Jesus, you are positioned by God to be a part of the rescue and salvation of others!

The fulfillment of the dream isn't about power, wealth or fame. If you have any of these, understand God has entrusted those things to you with His purpose in mind. The goal isn't to chase a spot in the "palace". The goal should be faithfulness and fruitfulness with the assignment that He has entrusted to our care. We must remember that when God blesses us, His blessings are for a purpose: to *be a blessing*. God's dream for Joseph wasn't for him to arrive at the palace one day, kick back and spend the rest of his life consumed with how blessed *he was*. The blessing was there so that he could be a source of blessing to people that were in danger of destruction from a coming famine. God was going to bless people *through* Joseph.

How does He want to bring blessing through *you*?

Promotions and positions, as great as they are, should never be our end goal. We are citizens in the Kingdom of God. His value system is different than the value system of this world. Jesus said that His Kingdom would operate *upside down*. He told us if we want to be great, serve. If we want to have, give. If we want to be lifted up, humble yourself. Self-elevation is not a fruit of the Spirit. As we live as citizens of the Kingdom and we experience blessing, promotion or elevation, we should embrace those gifts as a means that God is using to accomplish His goal.

This requires a shift in our focus. As we look back over his life, Joseph's focus of his dreams change.

When he was young you can see his focus: *"I...I...I..."*

When he was in prison, it was a little less about him: ***"God can...But don't forget about me"***

When he reached the palace, he understood: ***"I can't, but God can"***

As God grew Joseph through the process it created a shift in his perspective and focus. I am convinced he does the same in you and me. Maybe you are in a season that God has given you a dream. You are excited, but most of the focus is still on you. Or maybe you have grown a bit to understand that it isn't just about you, but you still battle with wanting the elevation for yourself. We all struggle and process through these emotions. No one is exempt. The process that God allows us to experience, however, is a tool that God uses to get our hearts, minds and attitudes back on the real purpose of what the dream is about: *others*.

All these years later, as Joseph is standing in the palace, he is a part of a bigger promise. This promise was bigger than the dream that he had when he was 17 years old. Joseph is experiencing the fulfillment of the promise that God made to him, but it is connected to God's Promise to Abraham – and ultimately fulfilled in Jesus. God made a promise to Abraham in Genesis 15 that was about blessing. But the blessing wasn't just for Abraham. It wasn't just for Abrahams family (which Joseph was a part of). No, this blessing was for the entire world.

Someday, through that family line a King would come. He would live the life we couldn't live and would die the death we all should have died so that by trusting in His work *for us* we could experience this blessing that God had promised. We could be recipients of the rescue and salvation that God has provided through trusting Jesus!

ONE MORE NOTE FROM THE PALACE

There is one more important observation that I think we should take note of from Joseph as he experiences the fulfillment of the dream. When the famine hit the land, soon his father's household ran out of food in Canaan. Hearing the news that Egypt had grain, Joseph's dad sent his brothers to Egypt to purchase grain so that they could survive. His brothers come before Joseph and bow to the ground to show him honor, not realizing who he was (Genesis 42:6-7). At 17 years old, little did Joseph realize this is what the fulfillment would look like.

Now imagine for a moment you are Joseph. You are the second most powerful man in Egypt. These are the same brothers who beat you up, stole your robe *and* sold you as a slave. What would *you* do? I know for me, I could think of one hundred different ways that I could get even, show them who is boss or even rub in the fact that the dream *did* come true.

Joseph does none of this.

Here is an important principle for us to remember:

> **WHEN YOU DWELL IN THE *PALACE* THERE IS NO NEED TO DWELL IN THE *PAST*.**

There were many people that Joseph could have taken this opportunity now that he is in the palace to get even with. But God has given him a different perspective. God has graced him to see things through a different lens. The *pit*, the *pressure*, the *prison* and the *palace* all have a different look to Joseph now.

All of these years later, as his family is reunited to him, he understands how and why God was using the process to grow and prepare him for the promise.

> *"You intended to harm me,* **but God intended it all for good.** *He* **brought me to this position** *so I could* **save the lives of many people.***"* (Genesis 50:20, NLT)

The promise and fulfillment was all about others. He could have held on to bitterness and resentment. Maybe today, you are holding on to something from your past and waiting for your opportunity to get even. I want to encourage you to remember – if you're dwelling in the palace there is no need to dwell in the past.

Think of all the people Joseph could have tried to get even with:

His Brothers

99

They treated him with incredible cruilty and injustice. They despised him, beat him, faked his death and sold him for a profit.

With Potiphar

When Pharoah elevated Joseph to second in command, it means that in that moment, Joseph would have become Potiphars boss. I wonder what went through Potiphars mind when he heard the news that the Hebrew that he had thrown in prison was now in charge?

The Cupbearer who forgot about him

Remember the Cupbearer who told Joseph that he wouldn't forget about him, yet he did? Maybe Joseph can teach him a lesson on what it is like to be forgotten about for a few *years*.

But Joseph doesn't take action on these things. He is in the palace. He doesn't have to be a victim of the past any longer. God was working it all together for good (Romans 8:28).

No doubt you have experienced pain in your past. Maybe people did things to hurt you. Maybe you were overlooked or forgotten. I want to encourage you with a simple truth:

Don't allow the blessing of today to be robbed by the pain of the past.

How do we do this?

Trust.

Trust that God sees what we don't see. Trust that He is still at work. Trust that even if you don't see the palace yet, or you're not sure if you will ever arrive that He is with you in the middle of the process. He is growing you. He is preparing you for something far bigger than you can imagine right now.

God welcomes each of us to be a part of His great rescue plan. The palace is not just about us, it's also about *them*.

Chapter 7: **Why does God allow the Process?**

If God really loves me, why was this journey necessary?

I have something to admit. I figure since it is just you and I, this is a safe place to do it. Are you ready for it?

I'm not great at being patient.

There – I said it. The secret is out. This shows up in a lot of areas in my life. One area that I didn't realize it impacted so much was the area of food. If you're anything like me, you enjoy *good* food. Not just average, thrown together meals. You know the type of meals that I am talking about, right? The kind that you savor. The kind that with every bite you are reminded that Jesus is good and He loves you (As I write this I am realizing that I am hungry and haven't eaten lunch yet…). Here is what I recently learned from my friend while at their house for dinner – good food requires an intentional process.

Up until last summer my approach to grilling was turn the heat up as hot as it can go, so we can cook it as quick as possible. Why? So we can eat right now! I didn't want to wait. But last summer I learned something. We went to a friend's house and I arrived in time to watch him prepare. I knew from his previous Instagram stories that we were in for a treat. He didn't just make his meals, he embraced a process for making them. I watched, asked questions and listened as he described having the right temperature. What searing accomplished before grilling. Why allowing the meat to rest was so significant. By the way – for my plant based or vegan friends out there, picture us talking about a portabella mushroom or tofu or whatever else you might grill. What I learned in that moment is the right *product* requires the right *process*.

THE RIGHT PRODUCT REQUIRES THE RIGHT PROCESS.

Our lives are no different. Maybe we wrestle with why God even allows us to experience a process. If you have ever wrestled with the thought, "If God loves me, why is he allowing me to walk through *this*?", you are in good company. To be honest, there are certain things in this life that will never make sense. There is mystery in life. Not everything makes sense. Not everything always works out the way that we planned. But we must remember that God *is* faithful and He doesn't allow things to be wasted.

IT SHOULD BE EASY.

One of the great lies that we believe is that things should be easy. The logic goes somewhat like the following equation:

I TRUST JESUS

+

GOD LOVES ME

=

EVERYTHING SHOULD BE EASY AND GO ACCORDING TO MY PLANS

If we are not careful, we can embrace a subtle but dangerous belief that it should be easy. Think about Joseph again for a moment. God gave Him a dream at 17. Using the logic from the equation above it would be easy to assume that Joseph should go from Promise directly to Palace. If it is a God-given dream, that's how it *should* work, right? But as we discovered, God was growing and developing something inside of Joseph. He was preparing him through the process. He does the same with you and me.

THE PROCESS ISN'T PUNISHMENT.

Sometimes this process is longer than it needs to be simply because we haven't learned what we need to learn yet. Remember: *there is a difference between God "teaching me a lesson" and God cultivating my character.* God cares about your character, not just the destination you want to get to. If I am not careful, at moments I can embrace a theology that says "I didn't get what I thought…God must be punishing me." More likely is that he is forging something in your character that is needed for the assignment ahead of you.

The process you are walking through isn't punishment. Remember the lessons that Joseph learned each stop along the way. God wasn't mad at him. God was preparing him. In the *Promise*, Joseph learned that God saw him and had a plan and purpose for him. In the *Pit*, he was reminded that he isn't alone. While he faced *Pressure* at Potiphar's house he received a master's level course in character and honoring what God wants above all else. In *Prison* he saw a God who will equip us where we are at and that even when others forget, God never does. At the *Palace* Joseph was reminded that we have a God who has a plan to rescue and bring salvation to the world that He loves – and He allows us to be a part of His great rescue plan.

Here is a hard truth to remember at times: God isn't in a hurry. If you look at the life of Jesus throughout the gospels, you never see Him rushing or stressing. In fact, in one account we read about Jesus is asked to help with an emergency situation with a man's daughter. While he is making His way there, a woman who had been plagued with a horrible physical condition for years reached out for healing. Jesus stops. Think about the panic in the heart and mind of the father with the sick daughter in that moment. I can picture what is going on in this dad's mind, because I am sure it would be a lot like my own:

"C'mon Jesus! We need to *hurry*."

But hurrying wasn't on His to-do list. Jesus takes time with the woman who was healed, then continues with the dad and brings healing to his daughter (Mark 5:21-43). Jesus was willing to walk through the process because He already was aware of the product. You and I can find peace and be at ease in this same truth. Jesus isn't in a rush. He is willing to bring us through a process of preparation. He is interested in the final product for your life.

GOD ISN'T IN A HURRY.

I'm guessing if Jesus was grilling a steak (doesn't that thought put a smile on your face?), he wouldn't throw the grill on high and rush the process of preparation. He has something far better in mind. When it comes to all that He is preparing for you, trust that His process is the right process.

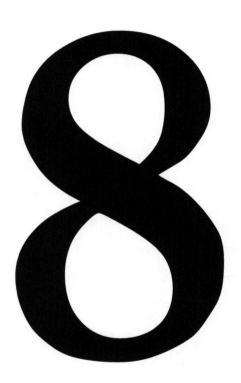

Chapter 8: **Your Promise and Your Process**

Making it personal

Years ago I had the privilege to serve as a youth pastor on the eastside of Seattle. Amber and I were youth pastors at one church for over ten years. We look back on those moments with such joy. Throughout those years there are moments that have stuck with me. Memories of time with students and leaders that have shaped who I am today. One memory that I will never lose is taking our student summer interns on a hike one beautiful northwest afternoon. I took these students on a familiar hike to me. I had done this hike so many times that I had lost count. It was special to me as well because this hike is where I proposed to Amber on September 21, 2002.

111

Rattlesnake Ledge has one of the most scenic views in North Bend. I loved the experience of coming to the end of the trail and stepping up onto a massive granite cliff with an unhindered view of the Cascades and the Snoqualmie Valley.

During this trip with our summer interns I was so excited for them to experience the view. The only thing that stood between them and that experience was a journey up to the ledge on a trail that was about a mile and a half long. As we started out on the trail there was excitement and joking. We were *all* having a great time as we journeyed together. But then the incline started. Within minutes the whining began. Soon kids were asking to turn around.

It created a perfect teaching moment. There on the side of the trail up to Rattlesnake Ledge I asked them a question: If the climb is so hard, why do you think so many people are willing to do it?

Silence.

Finally one student spoke up, "It's probably because they know the view is *worth it.*" Exactly! I took that moment to talk about the journey of faith. So many people throw in the towel too soon because it seems difficult or hard. Many people want the experience of the view without the investment of the climb. But for those who have a glimpse of what the view will be, they press ahead. Step after step. Breath after breath. They journey is worth it because they have a glimpse of where this is all headed.

> # MANY PEOPLE WANT THE EXPERIENCE OF THE VIEW WITHOUT THE INVESTMENT OF THE CLIMB.

As we have journeyed with our young friend Joseph through his process, my hope is that you have taken time to think about your own journey and where you are at.

Maybe you are in one of the darkest and hardest seasons of your life.

Keep going

Maybe you feel like the pit you're currently in is your final destination.

Keep going

Maybe your convinced it should be easier than this.

Keep going

Maybe the pressure that you are up against has you questioning the goodness and faithfulness of God.

Keep going

Maybe you feel like there are prison bars all around and you wonder how you ended up here.

Keep going

You were created for a purpose and I believe God has a sense of *Promise* for your life. Do you know what that is? Did you toss it aside years ago, convinced that it wasn't for you any longer because of the journey your life has been in? Maybe today is the day that you pick that sense of promise back up. The promise that God has for you is connected to His purpose. Don't count yourself out. Don't disqualify what Jesus has qualified.

As you consider your *Promise* and your *Process* and how God is growing and preparing you through it all, here are a few reflection questions for you to consider. I would love for you, as this book comes to a conclusion, to take some time to reflect. Maybe you want to grab a cup of coffee (I am a firm believer that we hear from Jesus better when we are fully caffeinated…) and a journal and take some time to get alone and reflect on what Jesus has been doing and what He desires to do through your process.

Questions to Consider:

PROMISE

Is there a dream, or a sense of Promise that God has given to me for my life? If so, what is it? Write it down and describe it.

What are the ways that I have been tempted to think that the promise is all about me?

PIT

Have I experienced time in the Pit? What was it like? What did I feel? What was a lie that I was tempted to believe that is not true?

Describe a time that you felt alone. How can you see now that God was actually with you, even in the Pit moments?

PRESSURE

When facing moments of Pressure, how has God used those moments to develop my character in ways that wouldn't have been developed without it? List a few specific examples.

How have moments of Pressure revealed what is on the inside, either for the good or for the bad? How do you think God wants to use those moments to refine you?

PRISON

Share a season of your life that felt like time was *wasted*. How was God using that Prison moment to grow something in you?

Earlier we talked about the fact that not every Prison has bars. What are some examples in your life where you lived "in a prison" that no one else could see? What did God develop in you through that season?

PALACE

How does your sense of Promise (your God-given dream) line up with God's greater promise and purpose to rescue and bring salvation to humanity?

In what ways has God been preparing you through the process for something beyond what you expected?

It was said earlier, "When you dwell in the *Palace*, there is no need to dwell in the *past*." What are some places of bitterness that you need to let go of today?

What have I been tempted to see as a detour, dead end or delay, that was actually a part of God's preparation plan for my life?

In what ways have I been tempted to avoid *the process*?

Chapter 9: **CONCLUSION**

I wish when I was younger I would have understood the journey that God would allow me to walk to prepare me and grow me for the Promise that He had for my life. The older I get, however, I realize that even if it was explained to me I still might not have understood or appreciated every stop along the way. God has a plan for you and He will allow you to journey through a process to prepare you to walk in it. You may have moments where you question. You may have moments where you doubt. If you do, it means you're a human. Keep moving forward and keep trusting Jesus.

HE IS FAITHFUL.

Remember that every stop along the way, if you allow it to, will prepare and equip you for what God has ahead. There have been moments where I didn't learn the lesson soon enough, so I had to stay in that part of my journey. The beautiful thing is that God's grace and goodness are always more than enough!

Keep your head up. Keep your hope up. Keep going. Where you might be today is not the end of the journey. Just because there is an unexpected detour, dead end or delay, remember that the journey isn't over. For those who feel like they are in their "Palace" season, don't lose sight of the purpose – it's about others, not just about you. Pits will come and go. It's not a matter of *if* you will face pressure, but a matter of *when* it will come – remember to keep your character. Prison moments are frustrating and disappointing, but if you allow it, God will cultivate something in you for the future. Allow God to continue to grow you through the process.

ONE FINAL NOTE

The goal of this book isn't to learn a few new things so that we can try hard to be more like Joseph.

Nope.

That's not the point.

Joseph's life is inspiring, challenging and encouraging. But true and lasting hope is never found in simply looking to a great example. We *all* need something more than that.

The ultimate point of this book is that we have a great rescuer who faced a greater PIT, PRESSURE AND PRISION than we could ever understand. He did it for our freedom and rescue. Even though we live with the reality of a great spiritual famine, He has abundance of food and He himself is the source of living water.

You see, Jesus is the real hero - Joseph simply points us to look in His direction.

Jesus alone is the source of lasting hope as we journey through the process and the preparation. His grace and faithfulness not only rescue us, they sustain us in the journey.

Now go embrace the *Promise* and *Process* – and watch in amazement how God is going to grow and prepare you for it!

Where this book started

A number of years back I was preparing to do a leadership teaching for a local school of ministry here in the Northwest. I couldn't help but think of the journey of Joseph and how important it was for young leaders to understand that even though there may be a call on their lives (the Promise) doesn't mean they are just going to arrive without embracing the process of the journey. From that idea, I not only wrote and taught that leadership lesson, but I also wrote a blog on my site (tylersollie.com). Here is that blog post from January 18, 2013:

GROWING THROUGH THE PROCESS

Problems and pain are things that I work hard to avoid. My guess is that you would say the same about yourself. When I start my morning and I think about my schedule and "to-do" list for the day I don't intentionally look for opportunity to add problems to my life.

Problems often bring pain. But they also give us a chance to grow, learn, trust and progress.

In Genesis we read about a young man who faced a series of problems:
He was his dads favorite and had really cool

clothes, so his brothers hated him.
His brothers threw him in an empty well.
(This makes me glad that I had a sister)
His brothers sold him and faked his death.
He ends up in Egypt and gets sold again to be
a slave.
His masters wife lies about him and he ends
up in jail, all for being good looking and
honest.
He helps some guys in prison by giving an
interpretation to their dreams, then he is
forgotten about.

*But the Lord was with Joseph in the prison and
showed him his faithful love...*

Genesis 39:21

Often our focus can be on
the PROBLEM when God is with us and
growing us through the PROCESS.

God walked with Joseph every step of the
way.
In the PIT
In the PRESSURE
In the PRISON
In the PALACE

Problems and challenges are going to come and go. The One who is walking through them with you will not; He is faithful. I'm sure that if we asked Joseph in the moment, he would have traded those challenges…we all would. Yet it was in the process that God was preparing him for what was ahead. Maybe without the pit, pressure or even the prison he wouldn't have been ready for the palace.

About the Author

ABOUT THE AUTHOR

Tyler is the Senior Pastor of Life Center (lifecenter.com), one church with multiple locations and multiple languages in Tacoma, WA. His passion is to help people KNOW JESUS and MAKE HIM KNOWN.

He and his wife, Amber, have 3 children and have also been involved in foster care. He loves good coffee, cycling, skiing, running and writing.

Connect with Tyler:

Blog:

tylersollie.com

Instagram/ @tylersollie

Facebook/ facebook.com/tylersollie

Twitter/ @tylersollie